WASTE MANAGEMENT: AT THE SOURCE

Managing Our Waste Series

Written by Erika Gasper Gombatz, M A

GRADES 5 - 8

Reading Levels 3 - 4

Classroom Complete Press

P.O. Box 19729
San Diego, CA 92159
Tel: 1-800-663-3609 / Fax: 1-800-663-3608
Email: service@classroomcompletepress.com

www.classroomcompletepress.com

ISBN-13: 978-1-55319-301-2
ISBN-10: 1-55319-301-6
© 2007

Permission to Reproduce

Critical Thinking Skills

Waste Management: At the Source

Skills For Critical Thinking	Reading								
	What Is Waste?	Pre-Consumer Waste	Post-Consumer Waste	Packaging	Soild Waste Disposal	Toxic Waste	Pollution	Waste and the Ocean	Hands-on Activities
LEVEL 1 Knowledge									
• List Details/Facts	✓	✓	✓	✓	✓	✓	✓	✓	✓
• Recall Information	✓	✓	✓	✓	✓	✓	✓	✓	
• Match Vocab. to Definitions		✓	✓		✓	✓	✓		
• Define Vocabulary	✓				✓	✓	✓	✓	
• Label Diagrams		✓				✓			
• Recognize Validity (T/F)	✓		✓						
LEVEL 2 Comprehension									
• Demonstrate Understanding	✓	✓	✓	✓	✓	✓	✓	✓	✓
• Explain Scientific Causation	✓	✓	✓	✓	✓	✓	✓	✓	
• Rephrasing Vocab. Meaning	✓	✓	✓		✓	✓	✓		
• Describe	✓	✓		✓	✓	✓	✓	✓	✓
• Classify Objects Into Groups	✓	✓	✓	✓		✓	✓		
LEVEL 3 Application									
• Application to Own Life	✓	✓	✓	✓	✓	✓	✓	✓	✓
• Model Scientific Process	✓	✓	✓	✓	✓	✓	✓		
• Organize & Classify Facts	✓	✓	✓	✓		✓	✓		
• Utilize Alternative Research Tools	✓				✓	✓		✓	
LEVEL 4 Analysis									
• Distinguish Meanings	✓	✓	✓	✓	✓	✓	✓		
• Make Inferences	✓	✓	✓	✓	✓	✓	✓	✓	✓
• Draw Conclusions Based on Facts Provided	✓	✓	✓	✓	✓	✓	✓	✓	✓
• Classify Based on Facts Research	✓	✓	✓		✓				✓
• Sequence Events					✓			✓	
LEVEL 5 Synthesis									
• Compile Research Information	✓	✓	✓	✓	✓	✓	✓		
• Design & Application	✓	✓	✓	✓		✓	✓		✓
• Create & Construct	✓	✓	✓	✓				✓	✓
• Imagine Self in Scientific Role	✓	✓	✓	✓		✓		✓	
LEVEL 6 Evaluation									
• State & Defend an Opinion	✓	✓			✓	✓	✓		
• Evaluate Best Practices	✓	✓	✓	✓	✓	✓		✓	
• Make Recommendations	✓	✓	✓	✓	✓	✓	✓		✓
• Influence Community	✓	✓				✓	✓		✓

Based on Bloom's Taxonomy

Contents

● ● ● ● ●　　● 　● ●●● ●　　●　　● ●●●

🍎 TEACHER GUIDE

✏️ STUDENT HANDOUTS

EZ✓ EASY MARKING™ ANSWER KEY

MINI POSTERS

FREE! 6 Bonus Activities!

3 EASY STEPS to receive your 6 Bonus Activities!
- Go to our website:
  www.classroomcompletepress.com\bonus
- Enter item CC5764
- Enter pass code CC5764D

Assessment Rubric

● ● ● ● ● ● ● ● ● ● ● ● ● ● ● ● ● ●

Waste Management: At the Source

Student's Name: _____   Assignment: _____   Level: _____

	Level 1	Level 2	Level 3	Level 4
Understanding Concepts	Demonstrates a limited understanding of concepts. Requires Teacher intervention.	Demonstrates a basic understanding of concepts. Requires little teacher intervention.	Demonstrates a good understanding of concepts. Requires no teacher intervention.	Demonstrates a thorough understanding of concepts. Requires no teacher intervention.
Analysis & Application of Key Concepts	Limited application and interpretation in activity responses	Basic application and interpretation in activity responses	Good application and interpretation in activity responses	Strong application and interpretation in activity responses
Creativity & Imagination	Limited creativity and imagination applied in projects and activities	Some creativity and imagination applied in projects and activities	Satisfactory level of creativity and imagination applied in projects and activities	Beyond expected creativity and imagination applied in projects and activities

STRENGTHS:

WEAKNESSES:

NEXT STEPS:

Teacher Guide

Our resource has been created for ease of use by both TEACHERS and STUDENTS alike.

Introduction

This resource provides ready-to-use information and activities for remedial students in grades five to eight. Written to grade and using simplified language and vocabulary, social studies concepts are presented in a way that makes them more accessible to students and easier to understand. Comprised of reading passages, student activities and mini posters, our resource can be used effectively for whole-class, small group and independent work.

How Is Our Resource Organized?

STUDENT HANDOUTS

Reading passages and **activities** (in the form of reproducible worksheets) make up the majority of our resource. The reading passages present important grade-appropriate information and concepts related to the topic. Embedded in each passage are one or more questions that ensure students understand what they have read.

For each reading passage there are BEFORE YOU READ activities and AFTER YOU READ activities.

- The BEFORE YOU READ activities prepare students for reading by setting a purpose for reading. They stimulate background knowledge and experience, and guide students to make connections between what they know and what they will learn. Important concepts and vocabulary are also presented.

- The AFTER YOU READ activities check students' comprehension of the concepts presented in the reading passage and extend their learning. Students are asked to give thoughtful consideration of the reading passage through creative and evaluative short-answer questions, research, and extension activities.

Hands-On Activities are included to further develop students' thinking skills and understanding of the concepts. The **Assessment Rubric** (*page 4*) is a useful tool for evaluating students' responses to many of the activities in our resource. The **Comprehension Quiz** (*page 48*) can be used for either a follow-up review or assessment at the completion of the unit.

PICTURE CUES

Our resource contains three main types of pages, each with a different purpose and use. A Picture Cue at the top of each page shows, at a glance, what the page is for.

Teacher Guide
- Information and tools for the teacher

Student Handouts
- Reproducible worksheets and activities

Easy Marking™ Answer Key
- Answers for student activities

EASY MARKING™ ANSWER KEY

Marking students' worksheets is fast and easy with this **Answer Key**. Answers are listed in columns – just line up the column with its corresponding worksheet, as shown, and see how every question matches up with its answer!

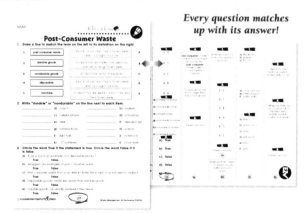

Every question matches up with its answer!

Bloom's Taxonomy

Our resource is an effective tool for any **SOCIAL STUDIES PROGRAM.**

Bloom's Taxonomy* for Reading Comprehension

The activities in our resource engage and build the full range of thinking skills that are essential for students' reading comprehension and understanding of important social studies concepts. Based on the six levels of thinking in Bloom's Taxonomy, and using language at a remedial level, information and questions are given that challenge students to not only recall what they have read, but move beyond this to understand the text and concepts through higher-order thinking. By using higher-order skills of application, analysis, synthesis and evaluation, students become active readers, drawing more meaning from the text, attaining a greater understanding of concepts, and applying and extending their learning in more sophisticated ways..

Our resource, therefore, is an effective tool for any Social Studies program. Whether it is used in whole or in part, or adapted to meet individual student needs, our resource provides teachers with essential information and questions to ask, inspiring students' interest, creativity, and promoting meaningful learning.

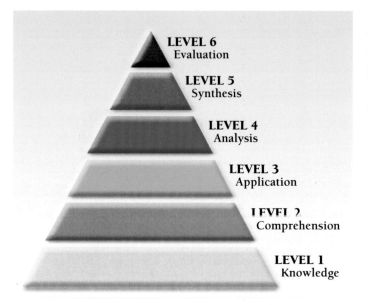

**BLOOM'S TAXONOMY:
6 LEVELS OF THINKING**

Bloom's Taxonomy is a widely used tool by educators for classifying learning objectives, and is based on the work of Benjamin Bloom.

Vocabulary

dispose	toxic	raw materials	manufactured	waste
packaging	solid waste	consumer	pre-consumer waste	post-consumer waste
environment	product	plastic	durable goods	nondurable goods
disposable	machine	petroleum oil	Styrofoam	atmosphere
ground water	acid	filter	municipal	landfill
incinerator	bioreactor	compacted	methane gas	radioactive
neutralizes	microorganisms	facilities	cross-section	hazardous
algae	algal blooms	bleach	damage	industry
contaminate	pesticides	fertilizers	pollution	pollutant
smokestack	point source	nonpoint source	runoff	mercury
concentrates				

NAME: _____

What Is Waste?

1. Complete each sentence with a word from the list. Use a dictionary to help you.

| dispose | toxic | raw materials | manufactured | waste |

a) The word _____ describes any part of an object that is not used.

b) You _____ of objects when you throw them away.

c) Objects that are made from machines using many different raw materials are called _____ goods or products.

d) The word _____ describes something that is harmful to living things.

e) Matter from the earth that is used to make products is called _____.

2. Match the product on the left to the waste that usually goes along with it.

1	cereal		plastic container	A
2	markers		bottle or can	B
3	soda		cardboard box, plastic bag	C
4	yogurt		tree scraps	D
5	notebook		cardboard box, plastic tubes	E

3. a) List _five_ things that are often found in your classroom waste basket.

_____

_____

_____

_____

_____

b) What do these five things have in common?

_____

What Is Waste?

What do you think of when you hear the word "waste?" You might remember a teacher telling you not to waste paper. Maybe you have seen a program about not wasting water. In these cases, waste means not using more than you need.

Waste has another meaning. Any part of an object that is not used is called **waste**. For example, think about what happens when you eat an apple. Some parts you don't eat, such as the seeds, stem, and core. These are wastes that you might throw away. The part of the apple that you do eat is digested, or broken apart, inside your body. But your body cannot use all of the apple that you eat. The parts that it cannot use are removed from your body as waste.

Describe the two meanings of the word waste. Have you thrown away any waste today?

_____

_____

When does waste cause problems?

In our modern world, the use of **manufactured** goods, or products, results in a lot of waste. Waste is produced during several steps:

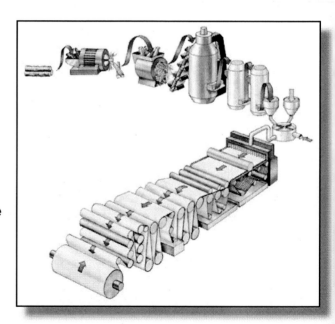

- getting the **raw materials** to make the product,
- manufacturing the product,
- packaging the product, and
- at the end of the product's use.

Waste from manufactured products can cause big problems for people and the environment. Unlike the apple cores, many parts of manufactured goods do not easily break down in the environment. People must find places to dispose of these wastes, but space is running out.

Some wastes may also be harmful, or **toxic**. When these wastes get into land, water, and air, they can harm living things. People live in the environment, not separate from it. In most cases, there are no completely safe places to dispose of harmful waste. Some of the waste often gets back into the air we breathe, the water we drink, and the food we eat. Finding ways to manage waste is an important part of modern society.

NAME: _____

What Is Waste?

1. **Circle** the word True if the statement is true. **Circle** the word False if it is false.

   a)   Parts of a product that are used up are waste.

        True   **False**

   b)   Your body gets rid of wastes as part of life processes.

        True   **False**

   c)   The packages that products come in are an example of waste.

        True   **False**

   d)   Waste is easy for societies to get rid of because of weekly trash collection.

        True   **False**

   e)   Toxic waste can be safely disposed of by burying it deep underground.

        True   **False**

2. **Put a check mark (✓) next to the answer that is most correct.**

   a)   **Which waste breaks down easily in the environment?**

   ○ **A**   a banana peel
   ○ **B**   a plastic wrapper
   ○ **C**   a used battery
   ○ **D**   a broken car

   b)   **Jana drinks a box of apple juice. Which of these is NOT waste from this product?**

   ○ **A**   plastic wrappers
   ○ **B**   the apple juice
   ○ **C**   apple seeds and stems
   ○ **D**   the straw

   c)   **Which of these wastes is toxic?**

   ○ **A**   tree scraps from a paper mill
   ○ **B**   a half-empty box of rat poison
   ○ **C**   an empty glass pickle jar
   ○ **D**   a broken ceramic plate

   d)   **Which of these is an example of packaging?**

   ○ **A**   a marker cap
   ○ **B**   an orange peel
   ○ **C**   a paper cup
   ○ **D**   an egg carton

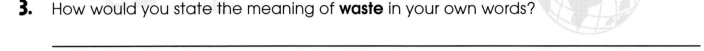

After You Read   NAME: _____

What Is Waste?

3. How would you state the meaning of **waste** in your own words?

_____

_____

4. Do all types of wastes create the same problems? Use examples to explain your answer.

_____

_____

Extension & Application

5. **Take a look at the wastes thrown away in your CLASSROOM.** Write a list of each item placed in your classroom trash bin for one day. Sort the wastes using the chart below.

Food Scraps	Packaging	Used School Supplies	Other

What is the most common type of waste that is thrown away in your classroom?

_____

Were you surprised by the amount of waste or the type of wastes thrown away in your classroom? Explain.

_____

_____

6. **Now take a look at the wastes thrown away in your HOME.** Write a list of each item placed in your household trash bin for one day. What are the three main groups of trash in your home?

_____

_____

_____

How does your household waste compare to the classroom waste? Are there differences in the types of amounts of waste? Explain.

_____

_____

NAME: _____

Pre-Consumer Waste

1. Think about the chair you are sitting in. How was it made? What raw materials went into your chair? What types of wastes were produced when your chair was being made?

_____

_____

_____

_____

2. Draw a line from the word on the left to its definition on the right. You may use a dictionary to help you.

1	raw materials		A person who uses a product	A
2	solid		wood, metal, rock, and other matter from the earth used to make products	B
3	pre-consumer waste		all of the living and nonliving things that surround you	C
4	environment		leftover material from making products	D
5	consumer		a form of matter that has a definite shape and volume	E

3. In the left column, list three products that you use in everyday life. Then, fill in the right column with the raw materials used to make those products.

Product	Raw Materials

Pre-Consumer Waste

What types of manufactured products are around you right now? Perhaps books, pens, desks, a clock. All of these things are made in factories from **raw materials.** During the manufacturing process, some of the raw materials end up as waste. Waste from manufactured products is often called **solid waste,** because it is made up of mostly solids, such as wood and metal scraps.

Many people think of solid waste as parts of a product thrown away after use. However, most solid waste is actually created *before* a product even gets to you! This type of waste is called **pre-consumer waste.** A consumer is simply a person who uses a product. The prefix "pre" is added to mean "before."

Describe the meaning of the word pre-consumer waste. Give an example of pre-consumer waste.

_____

_____

What happens to pre-consumer waste?

For every ton of waste that people throw away after they buy products, twenty tons of waste was made to make those products. Finding a place to dispose of pre-consumer waste from factories can be a problem. Long ago, factories used to dump large amounts of solid waste into the environment. Now, stricter laws control how this waste must be disposed.

Getting raw materials can be costly and harmful to the environment. For example, metal mines need expensive machinery to operate. Large areas of land must be moved, and the area becomes unsuitable for many plants and animals.

When manufacturing first began, raw materials seemed plentiful. Land and space for wildlife also seemed plentiful. Pre-consumer waste was often simply thrown away. Now, things are changing. Raw materials are harder to find and more expensive to get. More land is used by people, so less land is available to wildlife. People now look for ways to make manufacturing less wasteful, and to save and reuse scraps instead of throwing them away.

NAME: _____

Pre-Consumer Waste

1. **Fill in each blank with the correct word from the reading passage. Words may be used more than once.**

Products are manufactured from _____. During manufacturing,

a

leftover scraps end up as _____. In fact, most waste from products

b

is _____. In the past, most _____ was dumped in the

c   d

_____. Now, _____ are becoming more difficult to get.

e   f

People look for ways to _____ scraps instead of just throwing them

g

away.

2. **Use the words in the list to answer the questions.**

before	factory	manufacturing	metal
mining	plastic	pre-consumer	wood

_____ a) Which raw material is used to make a bicycle frame?

_____ b) How do people get metals from the earth?

_____ c) Which raw material is used to make paper?

_____ d) What type of waste is made before you buy a product?

_____ e) When water bottles are manufactured, what type of

                                    pre-consumer waste is produced?

_____ f) What does the prefix "pre" mean when added to a word?

_____ g) What is the process by which products are made from

                                    many different materials?

_____ h) What is the name of a place that manufactures goods?

Pre-Consumer Waste

3. Fill in the flow chart below to show **how a notebook is made.** Begin by describing how people get the raw materials. Then, describe how the materials are made into the notebook. List the pre-consumer waste that is created during each process. Describe how the notebook gets from the factory to you.

Pre-consumer waste	**Pre-consumer waste**

1. Getting the raw materials	**2. Making the notebook**	**3. Delivering the notebook**

4. You buy the notebook in a store.

Extension & Application

4. **Design a brochure** which will convince factories to lessen the amount of pre-consumer waste they produce. Choose any product, and write your brochure to the factory that makes that product.

In your brochure, be sure to include:

- information about the raw materials used in your product
- the benefits to the factory of using fewer raw materials
- ways that they can save raw materials, or use less to make the same amount of product

NAME: _____

Post-Consumer Waste

1. Use a dictionary to look up the words DURABLE and DISPOSABLE. Write the definitions on the lines below.

a) The definition of **durable** is:

_____

_____

b) The definition of **disposable** is:

_____

_____

2. a) Think of **ten** things that you threw away in the past day or two. Describe those things on the lines below.

1) _____

2) _____

3) _____

4) _____

5) _____

6) _____

7) _____

8) _____

9) _____

10) _____

b) Circle all of the things on your list that were **disposable.**

Make a star next to the things on your list that you used more than once before throwing away.

Post-Consumer Waste

What happens after a product is no longer useful? Batteries run out. Music players break. Pens run out of ink. After you use a product, most or all of it becomes waste. This type of waste is called **post-consumer waste.** The prefix "post" is used to mean "after."

Post-consumer waste is any waste from a product *after* you buy it in a store. Wrappers, containers, and parts of the product that are thrown away after its use are all post-consumer waste.

Describe the meaning of the word post-consumer waste. What types of post-consumer waste are produced when you buy a box of markers?

_____

_____

What are some types of post-consumer waste?

The amount and type of post-consumer waste differs from product to product. Some machines, like refrigerators and cars, can be used for many years. These **durable goods** can often be fixed many times if some of their parts break. When they finally reach the end of their useful life, some of their parts can be taken off and used for other machines. Some of the metal waste from these machines can be melted and made into new parts.

Many of the smaller products that you use every day are called **nondurable goods.** These are products that you use for a little while and then throw away. Examples of nondurable goods include pens, notebooks, and game cartridges. Once they are broken or used up, they become waste.

Some nondurable goods are made to be used only once and then thrown away. These **disposable** goods include paper cups, napkins, and plastic baggies. Disposable goods are easy to use, because they do not have to be cleaned or taken care of. However, they become waste after only one use. This creates problems because communities are running out of room to put all of their waste.

Post-Consumer Waste

1. Draw a line to match the term on the left to its definition on the right.

1 post-consumer waste	a mechanical device used in the performance of some type of work	**A**
2 durable goods	products that are made to be used only once before being thrown away	**B**
3 nondurable goods	products that last for many years	**C**
4 disposable	any part of a product that is thrown away after it is bought in a store	**D**
5 machine	products that are used for a short time and then thrown away	**E**

2. Write "durable" or "nondurable" on the line next to each item.

_____ **a)** couch   _____ **b)** markers

_____ **c)** cellular phone   _____ **d)** school bus

_____ **e)** desk   _____ **f)** television set

_____ **g)** running shoes   _____ **h)** scissors

_____ **i)** light bulb   _____ **j)** notebook

_____ **k)** "D" batteries   _____ **l)** book shelf

3. Circle the word True if the statement is true. Circle the word False if it is false.

a) A juice box is an example of a disposable product.

    True   **False**

b) Wrappers are examples of post-consumer waste.

    True   **False**

c) Post-consumer waste from your desk includes the scraps of wood used to make it.

    True   **False**

d) Disposable goods create less waste than durable goods.

    True   **False**

e) Durable goods can usually be fixed if they break.

    True   **False**

Post-Consumer Waste

4. Explain the difference between **pre-consumer waste** and **post-consumer waste.**

_____

_____

5. Explain the difference between **durable goods** and **nondurable goods.**

_____

_____

Extension & Application

6. **Keep track of your post-consumer waste.** Use the chart below to classify everything you throw away for one week. Multiple use items are products that you use more than one time before throwing them away.

DURABLE	NONDURABLE	
	Multiple Use	Disposable

Which column had the most entries after one week? _____

Brainstorm a list of ways that you could lessen the amount of disposable waste that you throw away.

_____

_____

_____

NAME: _____

Packaging

1. Write a definition for the word **packaging** on the lines below. You may use a dictionary to help you.

_____

_____

2. Draw a line to match the products on the left to their usual packaging on the right.

1	milk	bubble wrap and a cardboard box	**A**
2	cereal	hard plastic case with a plastic wrapper	**B**
3	DVD	waxed paper carton	**C**
4	picture frame	thin metal tube with a plastic cap inside of a cardboard box	**D**
5	toothpaste	glass jar with a metal lid and paper label	**E**
6	jam	plastic bag inside of a cardboard box	**F**

3. On the lines below, describe **five** examples of packaging waste that you threw away in the past couple days.

_____

_____

_____

_____

_____

Packaging

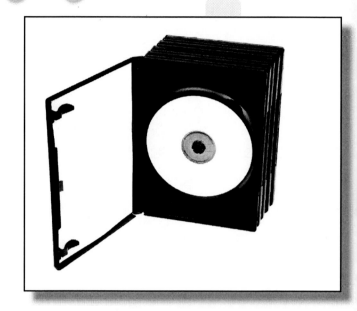

Think about walking down the aisles of a store. What do you see? Usually, you see boxes, cans, and other types of packages. Materials that contain or protect products are called **packaging.** A product's packaging may be as simple as a label or a wrapper. Some products have very large packages made of many different types of materials, such as plastic, Styrofoam, and cardboard.

Packages have many purposes. Labels advertise a brand and provide information about contents. Labels let you tell one type of milk from another, for example; Boxes and bags contain loose materials, such as cereal and flour. Bottles keep liquid products contained. Electronics like video games often have packages that are much larger than the actual product. These packages protect easily breakable products.

What is packaging? Describe different ways juices are packaged.

_____

_____

Why does packaging cause problems?

Like products themselves, packaging must be manufactured from raw materials. Trees must be cut to make paper labels and cardboard boxes. Tin must be mined to make cans. **Plastics,** made from **petroleum oil,** must be produced for many types of packaging materials.

The manufacturing of packaging has the same problems as the manufacturing of goods. Getting raw materials is costly and can be harmful to the environment. More pre-consumer waste is created during the manufacturing process. Packaging also creates more post-consumer waste, because it is simply thrown away when a product is purchased. Heavy or bulky packaging is more difficult to transport to stores. It requires more trucks to transport products with larger packages. More trucks create more pollution, and more cost for the product.

NAME: _____

After You Read 📖

Packaging

1. Use the words from the list to label each type of packaging.

glass jar	plastic bottle	tin can
Styrofoam	plastic wrapper	cardboard box

a) _____

b) _____

c) _____

d) _____

e) _____

f) _____

2. Write the raw material next to the packaging that was made from it. You may use each raw materials more than once.

glass	metal	petroleum oil	trees

_____ **a)** cardboard box _____ **b)** plastic wrapper

_____ **c)** can _____ **d)** Styrofoam

_____ **e)** paper label _____ **f)** jar

© CLASSROOM COMPLETE PRESS

21

Waste Management: At the Source CC5764

After You Read 📖

Packaging

3. Explain **two** reasons why packaging adds cost to a product.

1) _____

_____

2) _____

_____

4. Explain **two** ways in which too much packaging can harm the environment.

1) _____

_____

2) _____

_____

Extension & Application

5. Design new packaging.

Think of **five products** that come in a lot of packaging. List those products below, and briefly describe their packaging.

1) _____

2) _____

3) _____

4) _____

5) _____

For each item on your list, draw a design for new packaging that uses fewer raw materials.

NAME: _____

Solid Waste Disposal

1. What do you think happens to your **garbage** after it is picked up by a garbage truck? Write your ideas on the lines below.

_____

_____

_____

2. Use a dictionary to look up the meaning of the word **disposal**. Write the definition on the lines below.

_____

_____

3. Match the term on the left to its definition on the right. You may use a dictionary to help you.

1	**atmosphere**	all of the living and nonliving things that surround you	A
2	**environment**	a material that removes solids from gas or liquid	B
3	**ground water**	a substance that can be burned to produce useful energy	C
4	**fuel**	related to a town or city	D
5	**gas**	the layer of gases above Earth's surface containing the air we breathe	E
6	**acid**	water beneath Earth's surface; the source of drinking water in springs and wells	F
7	**filter**	a substance that makes water taste sour and causes some materials to break down	G
8	**municipal**	matter that does not have a definite shape or volume	H

Solid Waste Disposal

D id you ever think about what happens when you throw an object in the trash? You probably know that a trash collector empties your trash into a large truck. But where does it go? Most of the **solid wastes** produced in cities and towns go to solid waste **landfills**. Landfills are special facilities that are built to contain waste in the ground.

A smaller portion of the solid wastes produced in cities and towns go to solid waste **incinerators**. These are facilities where solid waste is burned at very high temperatures. Fewer solids are left after burning. Therefore, burning reduces, or lessens, the amount of solid waste that must be buried.

Describe two different places that your trash can go when it is collected at the street.

_____

_____

How do landfills work?

There are different types of landfills. Waste from homes and schools goes to a *municipal solid waste landfill.* These landfills have strict government requirements to help prevent wastes from getting into the environment. The bottom and sides of the landfills have special liners that stop waste from getting into the soil or groundwater. Waste piles at landfills are **compacted**, or pressed down, by large machines. Any liquid that seeps out of the waste is collected and treated to remove harmful substances. Scientists frequently test the soil and water around landfills to be sure no wastes are leaking into the environment.

When waste breaks down in landfills, **methane gas** is produced. Methane gas can have harmful effects in the atmosphere. However, it can also be burned for fuel. Many newer landfills collect the methane gas and pipe it to locations where it is used as a fuel source.

NAME: _____

 After You Read

Solid Waste Disposal

1. Fill in each blank with the correct word from the list below.

landfill	incinerator	methane gas	bioreactor
radioactive	neutralizes	microorganisms	compacted

a) A(n) [_____] is a facility in which solid waste is buried.

b) Some solid waste is burned in a(n) [_____].

c) In landfills, the breakdown of solid waste produces [_____], which can be collected and used for fuel.

d) A(n) [_____] is a type of landfill that breaks down waste from once-living things.

e) [_____] waste breaks down and releases a type of energy that is harmful to living things.

f) Smokestack scrubbers spray liquid that [_____] acids in the smoke.

g) Tiny living things are sometimes called [_____].

h) In landfills, piles of trash are [_____], or pressed down, by large machines.

2. Number the events from 1 to 6 in the order they occur in solid waste disposal.

_____ **a)** Garbage trucks bring trash to a municipal solid waste landfill.

_____ **b)** People put trash cans at the road side.

_____ **c)** Large machines compact the trash.

_____ **d)** People throw away wastes into a trash can.

_____ **e)** Methane gas is collected and used for fuel.

_____ **f)** Garbage trucks collect the trash.

Solid Waste Disposal

3. Explain how fuel can be made in the following facilities:

   a) landfills: _____

   _____

   b) incinerators: _____

   _____

4. Explain why it is important for landfills to be lined.

   _____

   _____

   _____

Extension & Application

5. Make a poster showing a cross-section, or cutaway view, of a landfill. A cross-section is a diagram that shows how something would look if you cut it in half down the middle. Be sure to show and label the following:

   - liners that stop liquid waste from getting into ground water
   - the piles of trash
   - large machines that compact trash
   - methane gas collection pipes

   You may use library or Internet resources to help you.

6. Research your municipal landfill or incinerator. Look in the phone book or Internet to find your local waste management company. Call or look on their website to find out whether your trash goes to a landfill or incinerator. Learn more about the facility that takes your trash. Ask the following questions:

   - What happens to the trash when it first arrives at the facility?
   - Is the trash sorted into different materials?
   - What types of machines are used at the facility?
   - What practices help stop waste from getting into the environment?

NAME: _____

 Before You Read

Toxic Waste

1. Do you know where your **drinking water** comes from? What would happen if harmful substances got into the source of your drinking water? Write your thoughts in your notebook.

2. The words **toxic** and **hazardous** are synonyms. Synonyms are words that have the same meaning. Look up the words **toxic** and **hazardous** in the dictionary. Write the definitions on the lines below.

   a) The definition of **toxic** is: _____

   _____

   b) The definition of **hazardous** is: _____

   _____

3. **Fill in the blanks with the words in the list. You may use a dictionary to help you.**

algae	batteries	bleach	damage	industry

   a) [_____] provide energy for portable music players.

   b) [_____] can be used to make things whiter.

   c) Businesses that all manufacture a certain type of product are sometimes called a(n) [_____].

   d) Another word for harm is [_____].

   e) [_____] live in water and, like plants, use energy from the sun to make food.

NAME: _____

Toxic Waste

Waste that is harmful to living things is called **toxic waste**, or **hazardous waste**. These types of wastes must be treated in special ways. They can cause a lot of damage if they **contaminate**, or get into, the environment. For example, if toxic waste contaminates a stream, it can harm the fish in that stream. It then harms the animals that eat those fish. People who use water from the stream may get sick, or else they must find another source of water.

Describe toxic waste. Define the word "contaminate" in your own words.

_____

_____

Where does toxic waste come from?

Toxic waste can come from many different sources. You can often find toxic substances in factories that manufacture goods. For example, toxic substances are used to clean machinery, whiten paper, and make computer chips. These toxic substances can end up as pre-consumer waste. Or, they can end up as part of a product. When the product is no longer useful, it creates toxic post-consumer waste.

You might be surprised to learn that many products you use every day can become toxic waste. Toxic waste that comes from homes is often called *household hazardous waste.* Batteries, electronics, paint, motor oil, pesticides, and fertilizers are common examples of household hazardous wastes. **Pesticides** are substances used to kill unwanted insects. However, many pesticides are harmful to other animals, including pets and humans. **Fertilizers** used to aid plant growth can be toxic in the environment. Too much of it can cause unwanted growth of algae that can harm water habitats.

NAME: _____

Toxic Waste

Certain businesses, or industries, produce a lot of toxic waste. Some examples are listed below:

- Automobile mechanics use many toxic substances, including motor oil, break fluid, and antifreeze.
- Hospitals have harmful **radioactive** waste from testing machines and cancer treatments. Radioactive waste breaks down and releases a type of energy that can harm living tissues. Bodily fluids, such as blood, and many types of medicines, must also be treated as toxic waste.
- Printing industries use bleach to whiten paper. Bleach can bond with other substances in the environment and harm living things. Some inks used in printing are also toxic.

Treating and safely disposing of toxic waste can cost a lot of money. Industries that must dispose of a lot of toxic waste usually have to charge customers extra money to cover these costs.

Describe how toxic waste produced by businesses can affect you.

_____

_____

What should you do with your toxic wastes?

It is very important to handle and dispose of toxic waste safely. The way you handle toxic waste affects your health, and the health of other living things in your environment. Never pour toxic liquids like paint, pesticides, or motor oil down drains. Don't leave old containers around. Some toxic liquids can cause the containers to break down and leak. Do not throw batteries, electronics, or other solid toxic wastes into the garbage.

Find out about toxic waste disposal programs in your area. In some places, toxic wastes are collected on certain days. In other areas, toxic wastes are collected at special drop-off sites.

Toxic Waste

1. **Circle** all of the liquids in the list below that are toxic waste.

spoiled milk	video game cartridge	hammer	ruler
old computer monitor	motor oil	fertilizer	batteries
T-shirts	wrapping paper	broken cellular phone	broken plate
candy wrapper	toothpaste tube	aluminum foil	glass bottle
paint can	lawn fertilizer	Styrofoam food container	glue

2. **Use the words in the list to answer the questions.**

contaminate	pesticide	radioactive	
bleach	motor oil	liquid	fertilizer

_____ **a)** What substance is used to help plants grow?

_____ **b)** What toxic liquid is used in cars, buses, and trucks?

_____ **c)** Which word describes toxic substances that release harmful energy when they break down?

_____ **d)** What substance is used to kill unwanted insects?

_____ **e)** What toxic substance is used to whiten paper used to make books?

_____ **f)** Which word describes harmful substances getting in to the environment?

_____ **g)** Which word describes a substance that can change volume depending on its container?

Toxic Waste

3. **Explain how fertilizers can harm natural habitats.**

_____

_____

_____

4. **List three things you should do to safely handle toxic wastes in your home.**

1) _____

2) _____

3) _____

Extension & Application

5.

Part A

Do a **household hazardous waste survey.** Use the chart on the next page to record the information you collect.

Go through **each room** in your home. In your chart, list hazardous items that are in use, as well as hazardous waste. Hazardous waste includes empty, old, broken, or unused items that need to be disposed.

Part B

After completing your chart, find out how to **safely dispose** of all of your hazardous waste items. Call your local waste management company or find their website on the Internet. Most companies have a special collection day, or a special drop-off site, for household hazardous wastes. Ask your parents or guardians to help dispose of your household hazardous waste. Keep track of hazardous items in use so that you can dispose of these items safely when they are no longer useful.

Part C

Use what you learned in the activity to **make a pamphlet** to teach people how to safely dispose of their household hazardous waste. Ask your teacher to make copies of the pamphlet. Give copies to students in other classrooms, your friends, and your family members.

NAME: _____

Household Hazardous Waste Survey

Hazardous Items in Use	Hazardous Waste

NAME: _____

Pollution

1. Has pollution affected you or your environment? Explain.

_____

_____

_____

2. Use a dictionary to look up the words "pollution" and "pollutant". Write the definitions on the lines below.

a) The definition of **pollution** is:

_____

_____

b) The definition of **pollutant** is:

_____

_____

c) Explain the difference between the meaning of the words **pollution** and **pollutants**.

_____

_____

3. Match the source of pollution to its description. You may use a dictionary to help you.

1 litter	can contaminate water and soil if it leaks	**A**
2 waste pipe	waste that is thrown in the environment rather than in a trash container	**B**
3 pesticides	allows particles from burning substances to flow into the atmosphere	**C**
4 smokestack	sprayed on farm fields to kill insect pests	**D**
5 oil tank	allows liquid waste from factories to flow into the environment	**E**

Pollution

When harmful substances get into the air, water, or soil, the result is **pollution**. Pollution harms living things. Sometimes, people think of pollution as something that happens "out there" in the environment. However, it is important to understand that *you* are part of the environment, too. You must breathe air, drink water, and eat food in order to live. If harmful substances, or **pollutants**, get into air, water, and soil, chances are they are getting into you, too.

STOP

Describe the meaning of the word "pollution."

_____

_____

Where does pollution come from?

Pollution has many sources. Hazardous waste can become pollution if it gets into the environment before it is treated. Some raw materials and products can become pollution. For example, cargo ships may crash and leak oil, which is very harmful to ocean wildlife. Burning fuel for energy is a common source of air pollution.

Scientists classify pollution sources into two groups: point source and nonpoint source. **Point source** pollution comes into the environment from a single point. Examples of point source pollution include smokestacks, waste pipes from factories, and leaking oil tanks.

On the other hand, it is difficult to determine exactly where **nonpoint** source pollution comes from. For example, the amount of pollutants in streams often increases after a heavy rain. Rain drains off the land and runs into streams. This water is called **runoff**. Runoff washes pollutants off the ground and into streams. Polluted runoff is especially bad in cities. The pollutants in runoff have many small sources, including fuel from cars, pesticides on lawns, and litter. But when they all enter a stream after a rain, they can cause a big problem.

NAME: _____

Pollution

How do pollutants get into living things?

Pollutants get into the environment in many ways. They enter air from smokestacks and cars. They enter the water from waste pipes and runoff. They enter soil from leaking landfills and underground oil tanks. But how do they get into living things?

Pollutants often enter living things at the bottom of the *food chain.* A food chain describes how living things feed on each other. Plants are at the bottom of the food chain. They make their own food using sunlight, air, and water. They also take in nutrients from soil. Animals eat plants, or they eat other animals that eat plants. When plants take in pollutants from air, water, and soil, those pollutants get into the animals that eat those plants. Then, the same pollutants pass into the animals that eat those animals. For example, pollutants taken in by grass move into cows when the cows eat the grass. When you eat meat or drink milk from the cows, the pollutants move into you.

Explain how a food chain works.

_____

_____

What can you do?

There are many things you can do to help reduce, or lessen, the amount of pollutants in the environment. Be sure to place waste inside proper containers so that it does not become litter. Never pour hazardous liquids down drains.

You can also join an environmental group. Some groups pick up litter alongside roads, streams, or beaches. This helps prevent the litter from polluting water. Some groups test, or monitor, water sources for pollutants. If they find high levels of pollution in water, they can work with other groups to identify the source of the pollution and help with cleanup.

Pollution

1. **Using the table below, classify the words in the list as point or nonpoint sources of pollution.**

oil spill	pesticides on farms	fuel from automobiles	
lawn fertilizers	litter	factory waste pipe	smokestack

Point Sources	Nonpoint Sources

2. **Fill in each blank with the correct word from the list below.**

pollution	point source	runoff
pollutant	nonpoint source	food chain

a) Pollution that enters the environment from a single source is called _____.

b) _____ washes many types of pollutants into the ocean.

c) A _____ is a substance that harms living things in the environment.

d) Pollution that enters the environment from many small sources is called

_____.

e) A _____ describes how one living thing eats another in a habitat.

f) _____ is caused when harmful substances enter the environment.

Pollution

3. Fill in the food chain diagram with words from the list below to show how one living thing eats another in a meadow habitat.

| mouse | snake | grass | eagle |

```
┌────────┐      ┌────────┐      ┌────────┐      ┌────────┐
│        │      │        │      │        │      │        │
│        │ ───▶ │        │ ───▶ │        │ ───▶ │        │
│        │      │        │      │        │      │        │
└────────┘      └────────┘      └────────┘      └────────┘
```

4. Explain how pollutants in air, water, and soil can get into animals.

_____

_____

_____

_____

Extension & Application

5. Design a poster to show school mates what they can do to lessen pollution. In your poster, be sure to include:

- Ways to lessen the amount of pollutants getting into the environment
- Ways to clean up pollution in the environment
- Contact information for environmental clubs in your school or community

NAME: _____

Waste and the Ocean

1. Imagine that the place where you live has a big rain storm. Describe how the rain that falls on the land makes its way to the ocean.

   _____

   _____

   _____

   _____

2. Write a definition for the word **runoff** on the lines below. You may use a dictionary to help you.

   _____

   _____

3. On the lines below, list **ten pollutants** that could be carried by runoff into the ocean.

   _____

   _____

   _____

   _____

   _____

   _____

   _____

   _____

NAME: _____

Waste and the Ocean

How does waste get into the ocean?

All through human history, people have used the oceans to dump waste. The ocean was an easy dumping ground. People did not have to look at piles of waste near their cities and towns. The oceans seemed huge. Many people did not think that the oceans could be harmed by the wastes humans dumped.

Now, people know that the oceans are greatly harmed by pollution from our wastes. Many countries have passed laws against dumping wastes into the oceans. However, a lot of pollution still enters the oceans from runoff, illegal dumping, and oil spills.

Describe two ways that pollutants end up in the ocean.

_____

_____

How does pollution harm ocean life?

Oil is very harmful to many ocean animals. When oil spills in water, the oil spreads out in a thin layer on top of the water. This layer often covers a very large area. Ocean mammals must come to the water surface to breathe. When they do, their fur or skin becomes coated with the oil. This coating makes it difficult to swim. Oil also coats the feathers of birds at sea, making them unable to fly. Oil also contains toxic substances which can poison animals.

Solid wastes, such as plastic bags and balloons, kill many ocean animals. Whales, birds, sea turtles, and other animals mistake these wastes for food. The animals often die after eating these wastes, which get caught in their digestive system.

Toxic wastes that reach the ocean build up in the bodies of ocean animals. These toxins pass from one animal to another up the food chain. **Mercury** is a common toxic metal in the ocean. It **concentrates** in large predator fish, such as tuna. Many fish are unsafe to eat because of the mercury in their bodies.

Fertilizers wash into the ocean in runoff. They can cause the rapid growth of algae, known as **algal blooms**. Some kinds of algae make toxins that are taken up by certain fish. You might see signs warning people not to eat shell fish during algal blooms.

NAME: _____

Waste and the Ocean

1. **Fill in each blank with the correct word from the reading passage.**

Throughout history, people have dumped waste into the _____.
a

Many countries now have _____ against dumping wastes in the
b

_____. However, a lot of _____ still enters the ocean.
c   d

_____ carries waste into the ocean after it rains.
e

_____ can coat the fur and feathers of ocean animals. Some ocean
f

animals mistake solid wastes, such as _____ and _____
g   h

for food. _____ can build up in the bodies of predator fish, making
i

them unsafe to eat. _____ in the ocean can cause harmful
j

_____ blooms that can be toxic to animals.
k

2. **Number the events from 1 to 7 to show the order of events that leads to a turtle dying from eating a plastic bag.**

_____ **a)** A rain storm washes plastic bag into a stream.

_____ **b)** People bring food to a picnic in a plastic bag.

_____ **c)** Deep in the ocean, a sea turtle mistakes the plastic bag for food.

_____ **d)** Plastic bag lands at the bottom of a tree.

_____ **e)** Stream carries plastic bag to ocean.

_____ **f)** Plastic bag blows away in the wind.

_____ **g)** Sea turtle eats plastic bag.

Waste and the Ocean

3. **Explain how litter thrown on land can hurt animals in the ocean.**

_____

_____

_____

_____

4. **Explain two ways that oil can harm ocean animals.**

1) _____

_____

_____

2) _____

_____

_____

Extension & Application

5. **Make a poster to explain why students should help stop pollutants from entering the ocean. Be sure to include:**

- how pollutants harm ocean animals
- ways in which pollutants get into the ocean
- ways that people can stop pollutants from getting into the ocean

Form or join a **clean-up group** to help stop pollutants from getting into the ocean. Your group can meet to pick up litter from beaches, streams, rivers, or parks. Be sure to have an adult help you, and find the right equipment to safely pick up and dispose of litter. Never use your bare hands.

Chart Your Waste

You will need:

- Mass balance
- Graph paper
- Pencil or marker

Set up a table like the one below.

Today's Waste

Description	Category	Mass, in grams

You are now going to **record each piece of waste you throw away for one whole day.**
Write a short description of each piece of waste, for example, "plastic wrapper". Then, in the
category column, write one of the following:

- packaging
- product

Products include all used or broken items, such as an empty pen.

At the end of the day, add up the total mass of waste for the day. Then, calculate the
percent of your waste that was packaging and the percent that was used or broken
products. Use the following equations:

> **percent PACKAGING waste = mass of all packaging waste ÷ total mass waste**
>
> **percent PRODUCT waste = mass of all product waste ÷ total mass waste**

Set up a pie chart to display your results.

Toxic Waste

Television News Report

Imagine that you are a news reporter for your local TV news channel. In groups of three or four, you will create a news report on toxic waste in your community.

BEFORE YOU BEGIN

Do you regularly watch the news? If not, spend some time in the evening watching different news programs. Think about how the news reporters are presenting their stories. What tone of voice do they use? What kinds of information do they present? How do they use visuals to help viewers understand the story?

DO YOUR RESEARCH

Together as a team, research one type of toxic waste from the list below. Focus your research on the effects of this toxic waste on living things, including humans and wildlife. Find out where most of this type of toxic waste is produced, and also how to safely dispose of it.

| batteries | radioactive | waste | motor oil | pesticides |

WRITE YOUR NEWS REPORT

Based on your research, put together a 15 to 20 minute news report. Be sure to include the following in your report:

- An introduction, which gives an overview of the information you will present
- Information about why people should be concerned about the toxic waste
- How the toxic waste harms the environment
- The sources of the toxic waste in your community
- Recommendations about what people can do to help
- Photographs, diagrams, and other visual information that will help the viewers understand your presentation

PRESENT YOUR REPORT

If you have access to a video camera, film your news report. Then, show the film in class. If you do not have a video camera, set up a table in your classroom and give your presentation live. Be sure to practice a few times first!

Pollution

School Action Plan

When communities have a problem to solve, community leaders start with an action plan. An action plan clearly states all parts of the problem, and steps that community members can take towards a solution.

Does your school have a problem with pollution? Work in small groups to write an action plan that you will present to your school community.

RESEARCH THE PROBLEM

Take a survey of your school's environment. Walk around the school grounds, and visit each of the buildings. In each area, note the following:

- litter
- hazardous waste
- pollutants that can contaminate air or water

WRITE THE ACTION PLAN

Summarize your observations from your research in a short bulleted list. Include photographs or diagrams that will help people understand your findings.

Brainstorm a list of ideas about what students, teachers, and staff can do to help solve the pollution problems that you found. Ask yourselves the following questions:

- What can people do to clean up pollution around school?
- How should people safely handle hazardous wastes?
- What is the best way to dispose of pollutants?
- What can people do to stop future pollution problems at school?

Write your ideas as a set of action steps. For example, "Assign students to help pick up litter in the cafeteria after lunch."

Present your action plan at a school board meeting, school staff meeting, or to an assembly of classrooms. Ask teachers and staff to help.

Product Life Cycles

Create a Diorama

You learned that products begin with raw materials. These materials are manufactured, packaged, and delivered to stores. Consumers then buy and use the products. When the products are no longer useful, they become waste. This whole process is sometimes called a product's "life cycle." In this activity, you will create a diorama to show a product's life cycle.

1. **Choose any product that you use in your everyday life,** from school supplies to games to packaged foods.

2. Collect the following information about your product:

*   What raw materials are used in your product and its packaging?
*   How do people get those raw materials?
*   How and where is your product manufactured?
*   What types of pre-consumer wastes are produced?
*   How is your product packaged?
*   How is your product used by consumers?
*   What types of post-consumer wastes are produced?

3. Use your answers to the questions above to **design your diorama.** Think about how to fit all of the steps in your product's life cycle into a shoebox-sized container. You may wish to use separate boxes for different steps. Be sure to include all of the following:

*   getting raw materials
*   manufacturing the product
*   using the product
*   pre- and post- consumer waste from the product and its packaging

4. **Construct your diorama.** You can use any materials you like. You might use foil, wood, clay, construction paper, glue, figurines, paint, etc. Be creative!

Present your diorama to your class. Be sure to discuss each of the questions in #2 during your presentation.

NAME: _____

Crossword Puzzle!

Across

1. used to kill insect pests
3. lets pollutants pass into air
5. _____ materials
7. containers, labels, etc.
9. waste from a product before it is bought
11. substance that tastes sour
13. matter that has definite shape and volume
15. rivers drain into the _____
17. place where solid waste is buried
18. manufactured item

Down

1. packaging material made from petroleum oil
2. type of landfill for once-living waste
4. harmful to living things
6. process by which raw materials are made into products
8. another word for toxic
10. parts of a product that are no longer useful
12. facillity where products are manufactured
14. facility where solid waste is burned
16. when harmful substances get into the environment

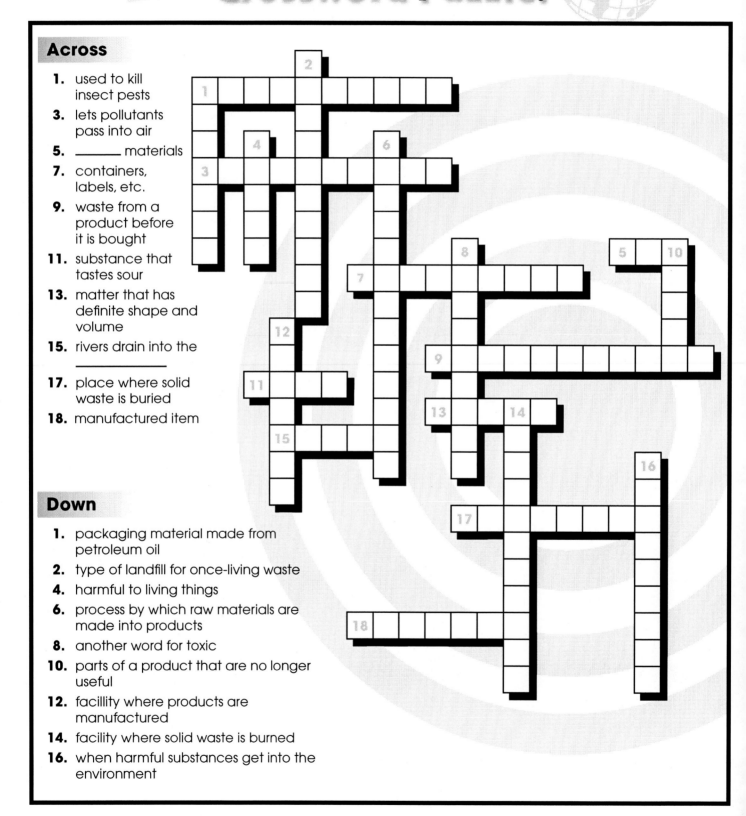

NAME: _____

Word Search

Find all of the words in the Word Search. Words are written horizontally, vertically, diagonally, and some are even written backwards.

toxic	pollutant	point source	neutralizes
disposable	fertilizers	radioactive	landfill
algae	raw materials	runoff	bleach
manufactured	consumer	bioreactor	styrofoam
nondurable goods	contaminate	hazardous	ground water
pesticides	packaging	municipal	microorganisms
solid waste	environment	incinerator	food chain

```
N A S D F G T N A T U L L O P S D S
I W S O L I D W A S T E E R Y A D Z
A E T L Z X E T A N I M A T N O C X
H T Y H A Z A R D O U S W T O I F C
C P R C V I B N J H G D Q G U X G I
D A O E F E R T I L I Z E R S B I N
O C F M F D G E B N H L A D H R P C
O K O N O F H C T S B K S F J E K I
F A A V N E U T R A L I Z E S T Z N
M G M Q U W Q M R D M N B V C A X E
U I S D R F G U I H A W J K L W P R
N N C M N B D S Z B L E A C H D E A
I G M R K N P I R U T R Q R E N S T
C A S D O O B E G H J K L R Z U T O
I Z X N S O M I C V B N U M K O I R
P Q W A E U R P O I N T S O U R C E
A R B T S Y U G I R C O P L K G I A
L L S N D F G H A A E Z X C V B D Q
E M O N B V C X F N O A L G A E E W
Q C W E R T Y U Z P I U C Y T R S E
E N V I R O N M E N T S Z T X C V B
R A D I O A C T I V E A M S O D F G
N B V C M L A N D F I L L S Z R J H
```

NAME: _____

Comprehension Quiz

30

Part A

8

Circle the word True if the statement is true. Circle the word False if it is false.

1) Parts of a product that you throw away are waste.
   True **False**

2) Pre-consumer waste is not as much of a problem as post-consumer waste.
   True **False**

3) Post-consumer waste is any waste made during the manufacturing of goods and products.
   True **False**

4) The usual packaging of toothpaste includes a metal tube, plastic cap, and cardboard box.
   True **False**

5) A landfill is a facility where solid waste is burned to produce fuel for energy.
   True **False**

6) The best way to dispose of paint, bleach, and other liquid hazardous waste is to pour it down a drain and run hot water for at least ten minutes.
   True **False**

7) Fertilizers used on farms are an example of nonpoint source pollution.
   True **False**

8) Oceans are so large that they cannot be harmed by human waste; therefore, they are a good place for dumping.
   True **False**

Part B

6

Look at the package of loose paper to the right.

In the boxes below, describe each type of waste made by the package of paper.

a) pre-consumer	b) post-consumer

SUBTOTAL: /14

NAME: _____

Comprehension Quiz

Part C

Answer each question in complete sentences.

1. What is the difference between **pre-consumer waste** and **post-consumer waste**? Give an example of each.

_____

_____

2. Describe two reasons to choose products with the least amount of **packaging.**

_____

_____

3. Describe what **toxic waste** is. Give two examples of toxic waste that you might find in your home, and tell how to dispose of them safely.

_____

_____

4. What is the difference between **point source** and **nonpoint source** pollution? Give an example of each.

_____

_____

5. Explain how living things in the ocean are harmed by **pollution** made by people on land. Give two examples to support your answer.

_____

_____

_____

SUBTOTAL: /16

EZ✔

3.

Pre-consumer waste: tree scraps, paper scraps

1) cutting trees

2) making paper, binding paper together

3) trucking notebook to stores

4. Answers will vary

⑭

1.
a) raw materials
b) pre-consumer waste
c) pre-consumer waste
d) pre-consumer waste
e) environment
f) raw materials
g) reuse

2.
a) metal
b) mining
c) wood
d) pre-consumer
e) plastic
f) before
g) manufacturing
h) factory

⑬

---

1. Possible answers: wood, metal; wood and metal scraps

2.
1. B
2. E
3. D
4. C
5. A

3. Answers will vary

⑪

Waste created before a product gets to a consumer. Answers will vary.

⑫

---

3. Answers will vary
4. Answers will vary
5. Answers will vary
6. Answers will vary

⑩

1.
a) False
b) True
c) True
d) False
e) False

2.
a) ◉ A
b) ◉ B
c) ◉ B
d) ◉ D

⑨

1.
a) waste
b) dispose
c) manufactured
d) toxic
e) raw materials

2.
1. C
2. E
3. B
4. A
5. D

3. Answers will vary

⑦

Not using more than you need, and any part of an object that is not used. Answers will vary.

⑧

3. Uses more raw materials, adds to transportation cost

4. Getting raw materials can cause pollution and take away wildlife habitat, creates more waste

5. Answers will vary

(22)

1.
a) Styrofoam
b) glass jar
c) tin can
d) cardboard box
e) plastic wrapper
f) plastic bottle

2.
a) trees b) petroleum oil
c) metal d) petroleum oil
e) trees f) glass

(21)

1. Materials in which a product is packed or wrapped

2.
1. C
2. F
3. B
4. A
5. D
6. E

3. Answers will vary

(19)

Materials that contain or protec- products; bottles, jars, juice bcxes

(20)

4. pre-consumer: created before a product gets to a consumer; **post-consumer:** created after a product gets to a consumer

5. Durable goods last much longer than nondurable goods

6. Answers will vary

(18)

1.
1. D
2. C
3. E
4. B
5. A

2.
a) durable b) nondurable
c) nondurable d) durable
e) durable f) durable
g) nondurable h) nondurable
i) nondurable j) nondurable
k) nondurable l) durable

3.
a) **True**
b) **True**
c) **False**
d) **False**
e) **True**
(17)

1.
a) able to resist wear; long-lasting
b) designed to be thrown away after being used

2. Answers will vary

(15)

Any waste from a product after you buy it in a store; marker tubes, cardboard box

(16)

3.
By causing the growth of unwanted organisms such as algae

4.
Answers will vary

5.
Answers will vary

(31)

Answers will vary
(29)

1.
Circle:
(video game cartridge)
(old computer monitor)
(Fertilizer)
motor oil
(batteries)
(broken cellular phone)
(paint can) (lawn fertilizer)

2.
a) fertilizer
b) motor oil
c) radioactive
d) pesticide
e) bleach
f) contaminate
g) liquid

(30)

1.
Answers will vary

2.
a) Capable of causing injury or death
b) Marked by danger; risky

3.
a) batteries
b) bleach
c) industry
d) damage
e) algae
(27)

Waste that's harmful to living things. Answers will vary.
(28)

3.
a) Methane gas is produced as solid wastes break down
b) Burning trash can be used to generate electricity

4.
So that liquids released from the waste do not enter the surrounding soil or ground water

5.
Answers will vary

6.
Answers will vary

(26)

1.
a) landfill
b) incinerator
c) methane gas
d) bioreactor
e) radioactive
f) neutralizes
g) microorganisms
h) compacted

2.
a) 4
b) 2
c) 5
d) 1
e) 6
f) 3

(25)

1.
Answers will vary

2.
The act of getting rid of things; throwing things away

3.
1. E
2. A
3. F
4. C
5. H
6. G
7. B
8. D
(23)

landfill; incinerator
(24)

33
1. Answers will vary
2. Answers will vary
3.
1. B
2. E
3. D
4. C
5. A

34
a) The introduction of harmful substances or products into the environment
b) Waste matter that contaminates the water or air or soil; something that pollutes
c) Answers will vary

When harmful substances get into the air, water, or soil

35
Plants take in sunlight, water and air, and nutrients from the soil. Animals eat those animals. Humans eat both plants and animals in the food chain.

36
1. Point sources:
oil spill, factory waste pipe, smokestack

Nonpoint sources:
pesticides on farms, fuel from automobiles, lawn fertilizers, litter

2.
a) point source
b) runoff
c) pollutant
d) nonpoint source
e) food chain
f) pollution

37
3. grass, mouse, snake, eagle
4. Answers will vary
5. Answers will vary

38
1. Rain water runs to lower ground, collects in creeks, flows to larger streams, then to oceans
2. Something that drains or flows off, as rain that flows off from the land in streams
3. Answers will vary

39
Answers may include dumping, runoff, oil spills

40
1.
a) oceans
b) laws
c) oceans d) waste
e) runoff
f) oil
g) plastic bags
h) balloons
i) toxins
j) fertilizer
k) algal

2.
a) 4
b) 1
c) 6
d) 3
e) 5
f) 2
g) 7

41
5. Answers will vary

42
3. Answers will vary
Answers will vary

43
4. Coating fur and feathers, toxins
Answers will vary

44
Answers will vary

45
Answers will vary

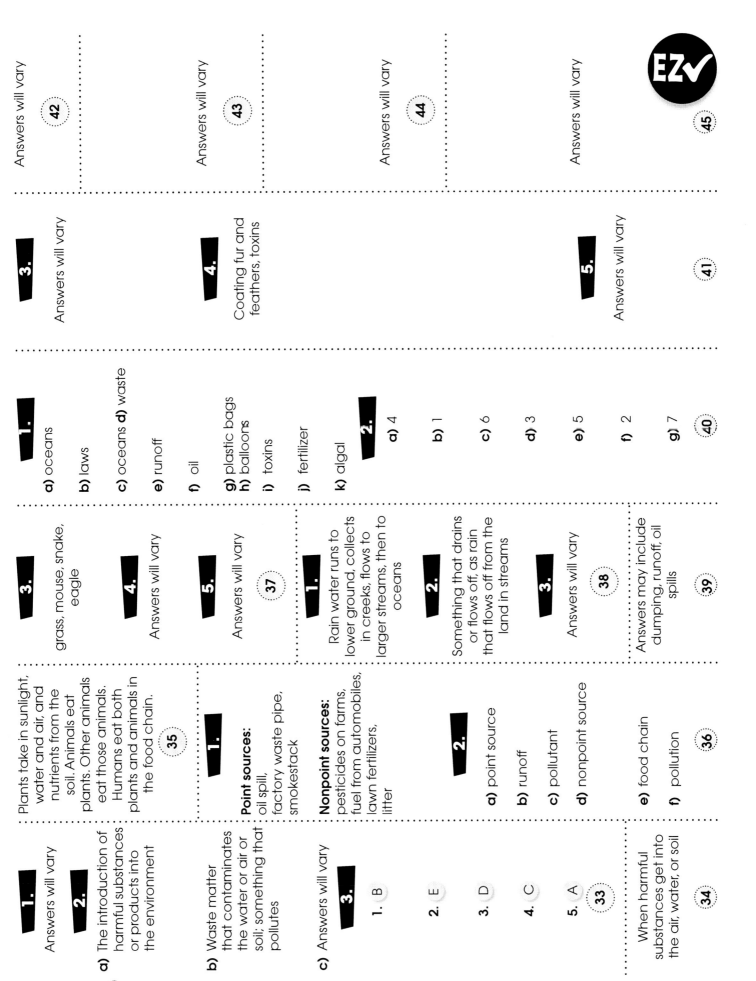

Word Search Answers

Across

1. pesticides
3. smokestack
5. raw
7. packaging
9. preconsumer
11. acid
13. solid
15. ocean
17. landfill
18. product

Down

1. plastic
2. bioreactor
4. toxic
6. manufacturing
8. hazardous
10. waste
12. factory
14. incinerator
16. pollution

Part A

1) True
2) False
3) False
4) True
5) False
6) False
7) True
8) False

Part B

a) tree scraps
b) plastic wrapper and used paper

Part C

1. Pre-consumer waste is made while getting raw materials and manufacturing. Post-consumer waste is everything thrown away after the product is bought. Examples will vary.

2. Answers will vary, but may include extra cost of making packaging, added harm to the environment of packaging waste

3. Toxic waste can harm living things. Examples will vary.

4. Point source comes from one spot, nonpoint source is spread out. Examples will vary.

5. Answers will vary.

---

46   47   48   49

Fertilizer Leaching

Beach Pollution

Shipwreck

Leak from Oil Barge

Chemical Waste

Pollution Control Barrier

Packaging

Canned Packaging

Gift Packaging

Water Packaging

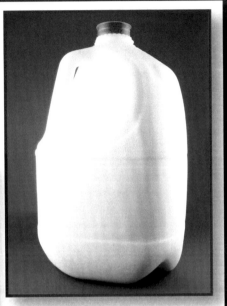

Drink Packaging

Fish & Chips

Fish & Chips

ish & Chips

Take-Out Packaging

Transportation Packaging

Waste Management: At the Source CC5764

Household Hazardous Waste

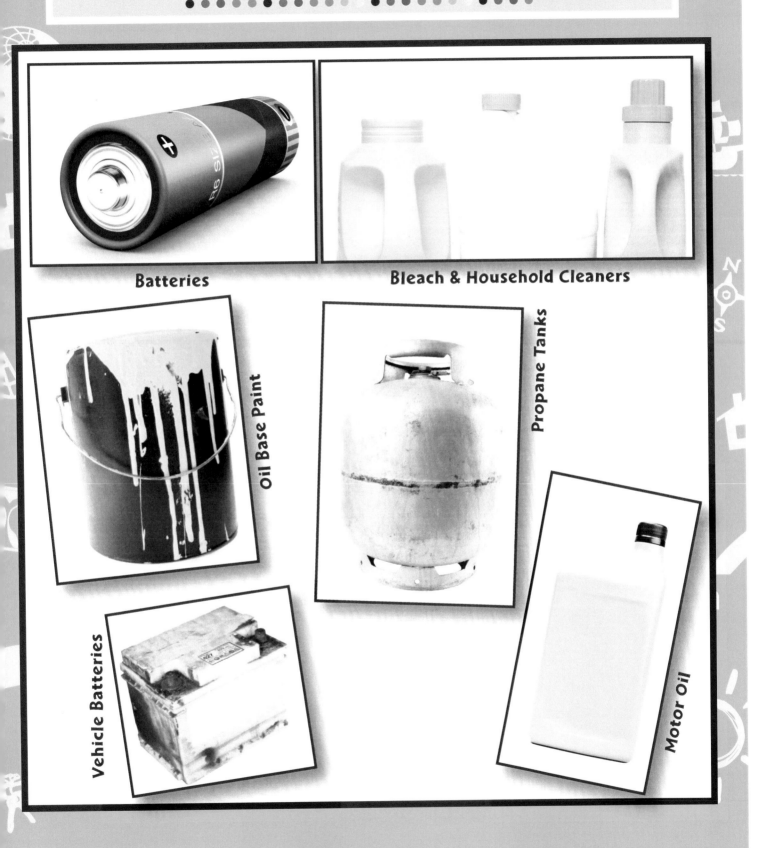

Batteries

Bleach & Household Cleaners

Oil Base Paint

Propane Tanks

Vehicle Batteries

Motor Oil

Point Sources of Pollution

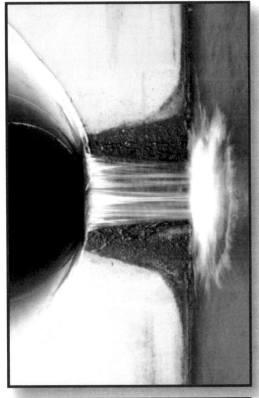

Factory Waste

Sewage Waste

Chemical Waste

Hazardous Waste

Non-point Sources of Pollution

Washing Oil & Grease off Driveway

Vehicle Emissions

Pesticides

Road Way Litter

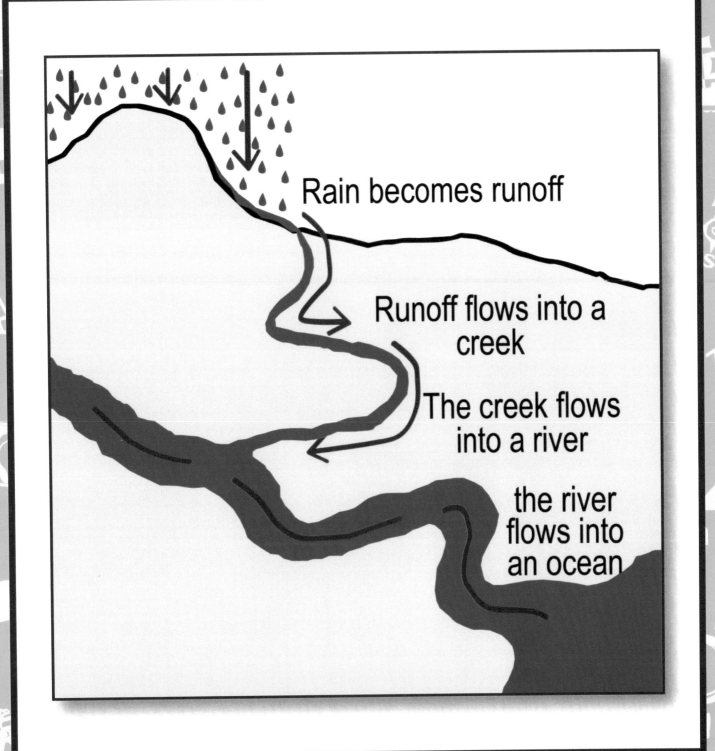

Rain becomes runoff

Runoff flows into a creek

The creek flows into a river

the river flows into an ocean

Publication Listing

• • • • • • • • • • • • • • • •

Ask Your Dealer About Our Complete Line

LITERATURE KITS™ - Books

ITEM #	TITLE
GRADES 1-2	
CC2100	Curious George (H. A. Rey)
CC2101	Paper Bag Princess (Robert N. Munsch)
CC2102	Stone Soup (Marcia Brown)
CC2103	The Very Hungry Caterpillar (Eric Carle)
CC2104	Where the Wild Things Are (Maurice Sendak)
GRADES 3-4	
CC2300	Babe: The Gallant Pig (Dick King-Smith)
CC2301	Because of Winn-Dixie (Kate DiCamillo)
CC2302	The Tale of Despereaux (Kate DiCamillo)
CC2303	James and the Giant Peach (Roald Dahl)
CC2304	Ramona Quimby, Age 8 (Beverly Cleary)
CC2305	The Mouse and the Motorcycle (Beverly Cleary)
CC2306	Charlotte's Web (E.B. White)
CC2307	Owls in the Family (Farley Mowat)
CC2308	Sarah, Plain and Tall (Patricia MacLachlan)
CC2309	Matilda (Roald Dahl)
CC2310	Charlie & The Chocolate Factory (Roald Dahl)
CC2311	Frindle (Andrew Clements)
CC2312	M.C. Higgins, the Great (Virginia Hamilton)
CC2313	The Family Under The Bridge (N.S. Carlson)
CC2314	The Hundred Penny Box (Sharon Mathis)
CC2315	Cricket in Times Square (George Selden)
CC2316	Fantastic Mr Fox (Roald Dahl)
CC2317	The Hundred Dresses (Eleanor Estes)
CC2318	The War with Grandpa (Robert Kimmel Smith)
GRADES 5-6	
CC2500	Black Beauty (Anna Sewell)
CC2501	Bridge to Terabithia (Katherine Paterson)
CC2502	Bud, Not Buddy (Christopher Paul Curtis)
CC2503	The Egypt Game (Zilpha Keatley Snyder)
CC2504	The Great Gilly Hopkins (Katherine Paterson)
CC2505	Holes (Louis Sachar)
CC2506	Number the Stars (Lois Lowry)
CC2507	The Sign of the Beaver (E.G. Speare)
CC2508	The Whipping Boy (Sid Fleischman)
CC2509	Island of the Blue Dolphins (Scott O'Dell)
CC2510	Underground to Canada (Barbara Smucker)
CC2511	Loser (Jerry Spinelli)
CC2512	The Higher Power of Lucky (Susan Patron)
CC2513	Kira-Kira (Cynthia Kadohata)
CC2514	Dear Mr. Henshaw (Beverly Cleary)
CC2515	The Summer of the Swans (Betsy Byars)
CC2516	Shiloh (Phyllis Reynolds Naylor)
CC2517	A Single Shard (Linda Sue Park)
CC2518	Hoot (Carl Hiaasen)
CC2519	Hatchet (Gary Paulsen)
CC2520	The Giver (Lois Lowry)
CC2521	The Graveyard Book (Neil Gaiman)
CC2522	The View From Saturday (E.L. Konigsburg)
CC2523	Hattie Big Sky (Kirby Larson)
CC2524	When You Reach Me (Rebecca Stead)
CC2525	Criss Cross (Lynne Rae Perkins)
CC2526	A Year Down Yonder (Richard Peck)
CC2527	Maniac Magee (Jerry Spinelli)

LITERATURE KITS™ - Books

ITEM #	TITLE
CC2528	From the Mixed-Up Files of Mrs. Basil E. Frankweiler (E.L. Konigsburg)
CC2529	Sing Down the Moon (Scott O'Dell)
CC2530	The Phantom Tollbooth (Norton Juster)
CC2531	Gregor the Overlander (Suzanne Collins)
GRADES 7-8	
CC2700	Cheaper by the Dozen (Frank B. Gilbreth)
CC2701	The Miracle Worker (William Gibson)
CC2702	The Red Pony (John Steinbeck)
CC2703	Treasure Island (Robert Louis Stevenson)
CC2704	Romeo & Juliet (William Shakespeare)
CC2705	Crispin: The Cross of Lead (Avi)
CC2706	Call It Courage (Armstrong Sperry)
CC2707	The Boy in the Striped Pajamas (John Boyne)
CC2708	The Westing Game (Ellen Raskin)
CC2709	The Cay (Theodore Taylor)
CC2710	The Hunger Games (Suzanne Collins)
GRADES 9-12	
CC2001	To Kill A Mockingbird (Harper Lee)
CC2002	Angela's Ashes (Frank McCourt)
CC2003	The Grapes of Wrath (John Steinbeck)
CC2004	The Good Earth (Pearl S. Buck)
CC2005	The Road (Cormac McCarthy)
CC2006	The Old Man and the Sea (Ernest Hemingway)
CC2007	Lord of the Flies (William Golding)
CC2008	The Color Purple (Alice Walker)
CC2009	The Outsiders (S.E. Hinton)
CC2010	Hamlet (William Shakespeare)
CC2011	The Great Gatsby (F. Scott Fitzgerald)
CC2012	The Adventures of Huckleberry Finn (Mark Twain)
CC2013	Macbeth (William Shakespeare)
CC2014	Fahrenheit 451 (Ray Bradbury)

LANGUAGE ARTS - Books

ITEM #	TITLE
CC1110	Word Families - Short Vowels Grades K-1
CC1111	Word Families - Long Vowels Grades K-1
CC1112	Word Families - Vowels Big Book Grades K-1
CC1113	High Frequency Sight Words Grades K-1
CC1114	High Frequency Picture Words Grades K-1
CC1115	Sight & Picture Words Big Book Grades K-1
CC1100	How to Write a Paragraph Grades 5-8
CC1101	How to Write a Book Report Grades 5-8
CC1102	How to Write an Essay Grades 5-8
CC1103	Master Writing Big Book Grades 5-8
CC1116	Reading Comprehension Grades 5-8
CC1117	Literary Devices Grades 5-8
CC1118	Critical Thinking Grades 5-8
CC1119	Master Reading Big Book Grades 5-8
CC1106	Reading Response Forms: Grades 1-2
CC1107	Reading Response Forms: Grades 3-4
CC1108	Reading Response Forms: Grades 5-6
CC1109	Reading Response Forms Big Book: Grades 1-6

MATHEMATICS - Software

ITEM #	TITLE
PRINCIPLES & STANDARDS OF MATH SERIES	
CC7315	Grades PK-2 Five Strands of Math Big Box
CC7316	Grades 3-5 Five Strands of Math Big Box
CC7317	Grades 6-8 Five Strands of Math Big Box

MATHEMATICS - Books

ITEM #	TITLE
TASK SHEETS	
CC3100	Grades PK-2 Number & Operations Task Sheets
CC3101	Grades PK-2 Algebra Task Sheets
CC3102	Grades PK-2 Geometry Task Sheets
CC3103	Grades PK-2 Measurement Task Sheets
CC3104	Grades PK-2 Data Analysis & Probability Task Sheets
CC3105	Grades PK-2 Five Strands of Math Big Book Task Sheets
CC3106	Grades 3-5 Number & Operations Task Sheets
CC3107	Grades 3-5 Algebra Task Sheets
CC3108	Grades 3-5 Geometry Task Sheets
CC3109	Grades 3-5 Measurement Task Sheets
CC3110	Grades 3-5 Data Analysis & Probability Task Sheets
CC3111	Grades 3-5 Five Strands of Math Big Book Task Sheets
CC3112	Grades 6-8 Number & Operations Task Sheets
CC3113	Grades 6-8 Algebra Task Sheets
CC3114	Grades 6-8 Geometry Task Sheets
CC3115	Grades 6-8 Measurement Task Sheets
CC3116	Grades 6-8 Data Analysis & Probability Task Sheets
CC3117	Grades 6-8 Five Strands of Math Big Book Task Sheets
DRILL SHEETS	
CC3200	Grades PK-2 Number & Operations Drill Sheets
CC3201	Grades PK-2 Algebra Drill Sheets
CC3202	Grades PK-2 Geometry Drill Sheets
CC3203	Grades PK-2 Measurement Drill Sheets
CC3204	Grades PK-2 Data Analysis & Probability Drill Sheets
CC3205	Grades PK-2 Five Strands of Math Big Book Drill Sheets
CC3206	Grades 3-5 Number & Operations Drill Sheets
CC3207	Grades 3-5 Algebra Drill Sheets
CC3208	Grades 3-5 Geometry Drill Sheets
CC3209	Grades 3-5 Measurement Drill Sheets
CC3210	Grades 3-5 Data Analysis & Probability Drill Sheets
CC3211	Grades 3-5 Five Strands of Math Big Book Drill Sheets
CC3212	Grades 6-8 Number & Operations Drill Sheets
CC3213	Grades 6-8 Algebra Drill Sheets
CC3214	Grades 6-8 Geometry Drill Sheets
CC3215	Grades 6-8 Measurement Drill Sheets
CC3216	Grades 6-8 Data Analysis & Probability Drill Sheets
CC3217	Grades 6-8 Five Strands of Math Big Book Drill Sheets
TASK & DRILL SHEETS	
CC3300	Grades PK-2 Number & Operations Task & Drill Sheets
CC3301	Grades PK-2 Algebra Task & Drill Sheets
CC3302	Grades PK-2 Geometry Task & Drill Sheets
CC3303	Grades PK-2 Measurement Task & Drill Sheets
CC3304	Grades PK-2 Data Analysis & Probability Task & Drills
CC3306	Grades 3-5 Number & Operations Task & Drill Sheets
CC3307	Grades 3-5 Algebra Task & Drill Sheets
CC3308	Grades 3-5 Geometry Task & Drill Sheets
CC3309	Grades 3-5 Measurement Task & Drill Sheets
CC3310	Grades 3-5 Data Analysis & Probability Task & Drills
CC3312	Grades 6-8 Number & Operations Task & Drill Sheets
CC3313	Grades 6-8 Algebra Task & Drill Sheets
CC3314	Grades 6-8 Geometry Task & Drill Sheets
CC3315	Grades 6-8 Measurement Task & Drill Sheets
CC3316	Grades 6-8 Data Analysis & Probability Task & Drills